WORLD winds

Meditations from the Blessed of the Earth

Edited by Earl and Pat Hostetter Martin
Foreword by Desmond M. Tutu

HERALD PRESS
Scottdale, Pennsylvania
Waterloo, Ontario

Library of Congress Cataloging-in-Publication Data
World winds : meditations from the blessed of the earth / edited by Earl and Pat Hostetter Martin.
    p. cm.
  ISBN 0-8361-3535-0 (alk. paper)
  1. Beatitudes—Meditations. I. Martin, Earl S. II. Martin, Pat Hostetter, 1942- .
BT382.W67 1990
242—dc20   90-43103
                                     CIP

The paper used in this publication meets the minimum requirements of American National Standard for Information Sciences—Permanence of Paper for Printed Library Materials, ANSI Z39.48-1984.

WORLD WINDS
Copyright © 1990 by Herald Press, Scottdale, Pa. 15683
  Published simultaneously in Canada by Herald Press,
  Waterloo, Ont. N2L 6H7. All rights reserved.
Library of Congress Catalog Card Number: 90-43103
International Standard Book Number: 0-8361-3535-0
Printed in the United States of America
Cover and book design by Gwen M. Stamm

99 98 97 96 95 94 93 92 91 90 10 9 8 7 6 5 4 3 2 1

To all God's children
who have discovered the Holy Grail
in rusty tin cans

CONTENTS

FOREWORD

Just before I was asked to write this foreword, someone in England sent me a card with a prayer I had never come across before. Perhaps it is a famous prayer that I should have known, perhaps not. Now you will see why I think it is a prayer we should use if we really want to get into the meditations contained in this anthology. I nearly said "beautiful meditations," but I think that would have been smarmy.

And now that prayer:

God our Father with your Holy Spirit
Open our minds to your truth,
Open our eyes to your world,
Open our hearts to your love,
Through Jesus Christ our Lord,
who opened his arms for us
on the cross. Amen.

Do you see what I mean? Yes, we need an openness to these images, strung together like hard jewels, to let them speak to us, to communicate their harsh truths.

We must not try to be too clever. We do not need to be too clever. We must just be receptive, open, appreciative, to smell the fragrance of the flowers, to feel the cold splash of the rain, to catch the familiar odor of damp soil, to see the ragged mother dandling her malnourished baby in rags. And maybe to be moved to cry, to pray, to be silent, and to let the Spirit inside us pray

with groanings that cannot be put into words. To marvel at the fact that poor, hungry people can laugh, can love, can be caring, can share, can nurture, can embrace, can cry, can whimper, can crawl over and die—that these tattered rags of humanity are Jesus Christ: "Inasmuch as you did it to the least of these my sisters and brothers." They are God's stand-ins, created in his image. They are precious, they have their names engraved on God's palms, the hairs of their heads are numbered, and God knows them, these nonentities, these anonymous ones who are killed and nobody seems to care.

They stand up to fight for justice and win, and they lose what they had gained. They have to shuffle back to beg for work, and have their children sell their bodies to keep body and soul together—ha, keep body and soul together. Yes, all of these, God knows them each by name. They are the poor, the voiceless, the ones who play an important part in our Lord's Beatitudes. He died for them as he used to be vilified because he used to sup with them and keep their company. And the world still seems to be the same. The rich are richer, the powerful grow more powerful, and the poor get poorer and more exploited and more voiceless.

No, the world is not the same. You are God's fellow worker, to be an agent of transfiguration, to change the ugliness, the poverty, the hunger, the hatred, everything

degrading. To transfigure all into their glorious counterparts, so that there will be more caring, and laughter, and joy, and compassion, and peace, and goodness, and affirmation of others, and they will feel good about themselves and stand a little taller.

Yes, God depends on you and says open yourself to be filled with his Holy Spirit and be still as you contemplate these images which will open your mind to God's truth, and open your eyes to his world and to his friends, the weak, the poor, the hungry, the homeless, the drug addict, the gay person, the down-and-out. And God will say to you, "Thank you for loving me in loving them. Thank you for serving me in serving them."

Isn't God wonderful? This omnipotent but weak God, this immortal but dying God? This God who waits on you and me to be his partners?

Amen. Thanks be to God for *World Winds: Meditations from the Blessed of the Earth* which help us to tune in to God's wavelength.

Desmond M. Tutu
The Anglican Archbishop
Cape Town, South Africa

EDITORS' PREFACE

Walk slowly here.

Godspirit is here.

You may find him among the Mataca in Paraguay. You may find her in a noisy Olongapo bar in the Philippines. Friends, it is time to untie our shoes. We are about to walk on Holy Ground.

This is a place of burning. Come, let us step aside and see why the bush burns. And is not consumed. Ah, when we broke bread together on that snowy night, did not our hearts burn within us?

This is a place of play. All the better with bare feet. But watch the ragged edge of that rusty tin. Did you know the Holy Grail is waiting to be unearthed in a garbage dump in Candeias? Need a hint? Unless ye become as a. . . .

This is a place of touch. The mud-red infant pats your cheek in Delhi rain. Here you embrace the Muslim mother in grief.

This is a place of dance. Come, get off that stuffy bus. Move with the joyful rhythms of a thousand feet dancing in danger on the warm earth.

Here, friends, we walk together with the Blessed of the Earth. The ones poor in spirit, the ones who mourn, the ones who are persecuted, the ones who make peace.

Here find inspiration and hope to continue your own journey of peacemaking, your own yearning to show mercy, your own hunger and thirst for the righteousness and justice of God.

Here you will enter the holy of holies with many different sojourners. Special moments of soul-eyes opening. Serendipity of the Spirit. Miracle amidst the mud. Grace in the garbage.

A Buddhist monk friend from Vietnam once wrote that people usually suppose a miracle is to walk on the water or in thin air. "But the real miracle," says Thich Nhat Hanh, "is to walk on the earth."

The writers of the reflections are not polished or professional authors. They are simple earthwalkers. People, like you, who thrill and weep at those moments when Godspirit—in the form of a child with a back cast or a beggar woman with a turkey bag on her head—comes up behind us, holds our eyes, and teases, "Guess who!"

The stories here often touched moments of most exquisite joy or pain for the writers. Jacobo Shiere, a Dutch worker of the Mennonite Central Committee in Guatemala, wrote us about the struggle for him of writing his haunting "Nu Cotz'ij."

"The battle is over now. I am glad, feel even some tears, and am amazed. How is it possible that you begin writing, do a second attempt, and then suddenly it is what it is! It is like I felt so often in my being an ar-chitect. The design does not take form if you do not start to draw the first lines you have in mind. I think this is life. Do what you can, not being able always to predict how and what will come out. That needs a kind of faith. Some people call it 'God.' Some people don't talk about it."

Sadly, we were not able to include here all the poignant writings we received in response to our call for reflective stories. We are grateful to all who shared. These stories have been written out of the daily encounters of Christian sojourners around the world, many of them with service programs of the Mennonite Central Committee. (Any profits from this book will go to those programs of MCC.) Most of the writers are North Americans, but we identify the country in which each meditation was inspired.

As you enter into these reflections, you may decide whether you want to read them in one sitting, or whether you would like to move more slowly. These stories are clustered under the banners of Jesus' Beatitudes, that shocking litany of the power of the powerless (Matthew 5:3-10; Luke 6:20-22).

Each entry is accompanied by a thought from Scripture, and we invite you to refer to the longer biblical passage indicated if you want to use these for devotional meditation.

These reflections have been written by and for people who care deeply about God's creation and God's people around the world. The writings here are not theoretical musings. Rather, they record encounters: person to person, person to God. They are stories with bodies: muddy bodies, bleeding bodies, bodies abundant of form. Incarnation! It is precisely here that we know the One who "took upon himself the form of a servant."

So come, friends, with awakened imaginations. Read here not words, but images. Images that take us beyond the numbing cynicism of mass media overload. Images that stir up the fires within. Images that awaken us to the burning bushes all around us. Images that help us catch the wind. For the Spiritwind blows where it wills . . . WORLD WINDS.

Earl and Pat Hostetter Martin
Akron, Pennsylvania

Blessed

are the poor in spirit,
for theirs is the
kingdom of God.

DELHI NATIVITY

Grey sheet rain
Delhi day
Migrant laborers
Huddle 'neath concrete
Jungle walls

Their mud, tin, sack
Falling-down shacks
Crowd 'tween concrete walls
For protection

Some there are
Who have no huts
The red mud wetness
Becomes their bed,
The red mud color
Their skin

Upon the crushed stone piles
The weary mud red mother sits
Cuddles her naked baby
On the wet streetside curb

The still innocent child
In celebration of being
Pats the smiling
Rain-streaked face
Of Mother
Tenderness and courage

She now
Madonna
Radiance of love
Despite grey sheet rain
Delhi day

Fern Martin
India

All generations will call me blessed, for the Mighty One has done great things for me. Luke 1:46-55

THIRTY CORDOBAS

As I left the supermarket and got in my jeep on a hot afternoon, I noticed that the girl who had said she would guard it was not to be seen. It just added to my suspicion that these kids try to take advantage of shoppers, especially ones like me who already felt guilty for having so much.

As often happens she came running up as I pulled away, expecting to be paid. "Where were you?" I demanded, my voice reflecting impatience and frustration.

Our eyes met. Hers were open, innocent eyes. "Oh," she said excitedly, but noticing my gruffness. "I was two cars up. The man there paid me a hundred cordobas!"

Her obvious happiness was inviting. "But I have only thirty cordobas to give you," I said.

"That doesn't matter," she assured me. "It all adds up."

"How much do you make in a day?" I asked, suddenly interested.

"Sometimes 500 cordobas if I'm really lucky."

"And what do you do with it?"

With shining eyes she said, "I buy some onions, tomatoes, and bread to take home."

I gave her my thirty cordobas and drove away. I had given her eight U.S. cents. She had given me a new perspective on happiness.

Ann Graber Hershberger
Nicaragua

The poor will see and be glad—you who seek God, may your hearts live! Psalm 69:30-33

SMOKEY MOUNTAIN

Jessie's hands are wrinkled like crepe paper,
burnt brown by the tropical sun.
His filthy T-shirt, ragged pants, and dirt in every pore
make him one with the people of the sprawling hill of garbage
that is home to the scavengers of "Smokey Mountain."

Rejects are Jessie's specialty.
In an instant, he can see the value of anything or anybody
as he makes his way over the smoldering rubbish
saving the discarded, the forgotten cast-offs of society.
A living made from the sale of cans, paper, and plastic,
is precarious at best.
But for the people of Smokey Mountain there is little choice.

The scavengers are living miracles of immunity,
not because they don't get sick and die.
They do, frequently.
The smoke is a slow killer—blinding and faintly toxic.
But many are able to trudge back and forth, day and night,
to continue their endless searching.

Many scavengers live for the big find.
They scrape and dig as if their salvation is there,
buried in the dirt and refuse of the garbage heap.
And when salvation comes, there is an unrestrained cry of triumph
bringing dozens of tattered women and children scrambling over the
              junk heap
to lay claim to a share of the big find.
Sometimes it is a gold necklace or a wad of money—
crumbs fallen from the table of the rich.
But shared it is, so more can live a bit longer.

Jessie is a leader, a healer,
a toucher of the untouchable, a friend to the friendless.
He is a son to the old, a parent to the young.
He can put color in the wind,
a smile on a face, a glow in the heart.
Jessie can be calm, angry, and loving.
His eyes carry a look that can burn up police on a roundup
or silence the pious do-gooders who come mincing to the squalor-
              ridden dump
bringing their soap cakes and sadness.

Home for the scavengers is where the picked-over garbage
has settled enough to lose its sponginess.
It is here where the outer walls of one shanty
quickly become the inner walls of another,
threaded below with small drains
carrying diseases from one house to another.
Home is a hive of driven humanity struggling to survive.

For all this, they have their wispy moments of joy,
a rare laugh, a clinging desperate love, a courage without measure.
And they have Jessie, who gives them what they long for most—
a recognition of their own self-worth,
a dignity they will never surrender,
an affirmation that lifts burdens, dispels shame,
casts off guilt and gloom, radiates the eyes, and warms the heart.

It is the likes of Jessie that trouble the rest of us,
dispensing his love with an easy smile, bringing sanity to the absurd—
being there, with them—the Blessed of the Earth.

Shay Cullen
Philippines

Father, Lord of heaven and earth! I thank you because you have shown to the unlearned
what you have hidden from the wise and learned. Matthew 11:25-30, TEV

ON SOLES AND SOULS

Feet tell you a lot about a person, about a culture. I remember reading in *Good Housekeeping* that a certain television star keeps her feet soft and smooth by slathering them with Vaseline every night and wrapping them in plastic bags while she sleeps.

I thought about this while I was staring at hundreds of pairs of Haitian feet standing in the dust on Good Friday. We were following the Stations of the Cross in the ferocious midafternoon sun, stopping fourteen times to remember the events of Christ's crucifixion.

An unjust verdict; the weight of the cross; stumbling; weeping followers; mean-spirited scoffers; the final torture, abandonment, death and burial. We stopped in front of pictures hung around the square as young people gave pointed and relevant reflections through a megaphone.

In front of the civil courts, for example, we heard about rigged trials for profit, when "judges say they're looking for justice and they're really looking for money." We stopped at the house of the magistrate, an official notorious for profiteering. Again the message from the megaphone was stark: "Christ carries a cross for all who are sick, hungry, cheated, or oppressed today."

Trooping around the square from one station to the next, I felt a truth I could not name until a priest said it later: "People here live Good Friday . . . every day."

Since my understanding of Creole was limited, however, my mind wandered from the megaphone to a new focus: people's feet. I saw that the roads and fields had worked their way into people's soles—a tough layer of dead skin and dirt that became a leathery shoe in itself. Some feet had sores; others, scars. Bare feet flattened from running the rocky paths were stuffed into plastic sandals, two dollars a pair, three colors, four styles, split, dirty, too small. Heels hung over the backs; calloused toes stuck out the edges. Sometimes the shoes were too big. One little girl's feet stepped midway into pumps that some mission-minded lady from the States had discarded into a relief barrel. My neighbor strutted by in five-inch platform shoes, modish ten years earlier.

Jesus washed feet that had pounded rocky, dusty trails for miles. He probably muddied the basin as he massaged the callouses and rubbed away the top layer of dirt. Looking at people's feet here, as opposed to feet in my culture where people go to excess to keep their feet smooth, I realized what a dirty job it was for Jesus to wash his friends' feet.

Foot-washing demands that we receive as well as give. A couple months ago, I stood in line behind the water spigot waiting for a chance to rinse my feet. Finally it was my turn at the pipe, which ran at a mere trickle. Suddenly, a woman kneeling there, waiting for her bucket to fill up, startled the life out of me. Before I knew what was happening, she had splashed water on my shins and rubbed the grit off my ankles. Then she turned her nearly full bucket upside down to give my feet a final generous rinsing. I now think I understand why Peter protested when Christ washed his feet. Her spontaneous act of kindness left me amazed as I walked away. I saw her put the empty bucket under the pipe to wait again.

Rebecca Dudley
Haiti

Now that I, your Lord and Teacher, have washed your feet, you also should wash one another's feet. John 13:1-17

Blessed
are those who mourn,
for they will be comforted.

NIGHT DUTY

You are sent to serve. But the favored servant is the silent one. You are sent to witness. But the best witness hears all. Before you can speak for Him whom the world did not accept, you must listen to those whom the world has not heard, and to the God who speaks through unknown prophets.

Campo Muslim is a little piece of swampy ground in the southern Philippines where Muslim people have sought refuge from the civil war in the countryside.

During the daytime, you could easily forget your task and busy yourself with programs and projects, talking with this or that person, running around town. Then night would come and the real work would begin. The work of listening. For it is easier to listen at night without the traffic of streets or mind.

One of the best places to listen is in a dark room with rats.

When rats circle your bed, petty concerns vanish and fatigue is forgotten. All you can think of is how many there might be and how to keep them from biting your toes.

Now you are fully awake and the other night sounds filter through the thin wood walls. Deep coughs choke from the old man next door; that miserable tuberculosis that won't let him work, now won't let him sleep either. His granddaughter, Mina, awakens and, remembering she went to bed hungry, cries out for milk.

The night seems to be filled with other sounds. "Body Language" throbs from the disco in town, jarring the night air. As the military who patronize the place return to camp, the music gives way to the intricate melodies of the eight-gonged *kulintang*. There must be a wedding planned for the morning.

It is particularly beautiful tonight. Perhaps Bapa Sakanda is playing. You are lured to the porch and then to the shadow of the bride's house. For a moment there is only the night sky and music.

Once the firing starts, you head home. The first time you heard the gun and mortar fire, it seemed to be coming from just around the corner. Now your experienced ear can identify the distance and direction by the echo, and what kind of gun is used by the sound and number of repetitions.

Last night the roaring hum sending a current through your bamboo bed meant tanks on the road. Tonight helicopters whirl overhead, bringing out casualties from the day's fighting.

The old man is still coughing. Mina's mother is singing to the child. It is raining a bit, and someone is pounding a board onto the leaky roof in the house next door.

The helicopters remind you of conversations you had that day and the day before. The stories come back. The girl in Marawi who is still looking for her brother. The pregnant woman whose body was found split open with a bayonet, the fetus ripped out and shot. The massacre of an entire Muslim village by government soldiers several years ago, which has never been investigated.

Your friend, Ali, who teaches in the Islamic school, told you about the massacre. Then he asked you the question that so many others have asked since you came to this country: "Why does your country send these weapons to kill us? Why do Christians do these things?"

I will lie down and sleep in peace, for you alone, O Lord, make me dwell in safety. Psalm 4:1-8

You started to say something about national security and then greed, but you couldn't figure out how to translate either one, and anyway it didn't make any sense. So you hid your eyes from him and said, "It is wrong. I am sorry." He nodded and you just sat together in silence.

But now your heart shrieks into the darkness—GOD! Did you hear that? Are you listening? I can't bear this all by myself. It is too much for my ears to hear and my heart to comprehend. Do you care about all this? Are you there, Lord?

Silence. Not even a dog barking. Tears trickle down to your ears. You roll over on your side. Sleep won't come.

Suddenly, a song pierces the darkness. No, not a song, an invocation. The cantor in the mosque intones the eerie beauty of the first call to prayer of the new day: "Allah Akhbar. God is greater. Prayer is better than sleep. Prayer is better than sleep. Come and pray, come and pray."

Peace washes over you. You let go a deep sigh. Oh yes, God is here. God is listening too. Thank you, God, for leading me to this place, to these, your people. Amen, Amen.

Sleep comes. Your work is done for tonight.

Patricia Wagner
Philippines

23

THE GOLDEN CIRCLE

"Oh Jesus, help me. Sweet Jesus, help me. Oh, can't you do something for me? Please!"

Jill's voice reaches me immediately as I turn down the fifth-floor hospital corridor. I hurry into her room and find her lying on her side, rigid with pain. Her sister Lena is leaning over the bed rail, trying to soothe her with quiet words.

Jill Robbins has terminal cancer. She is well into her sixties, with five grown children scattered now from Texas to D.C., far away from their mother in Harlan County, Kentucky. As a new volunteer with the community hospice, I have never before been so closely connected to a dying person.

I have trouble listening. It seems I'm always so busy formulating solutions or answering people's problems that it is hard to stop and listen. But when I hold Jill's hand, I am utterly helpless to lift the awful pain. I can only be in that place, awkward and frustrated, but present. That presence, I discover, is enough. It is precisely what Jill needs to carry her through the time of waiting.

"God, help me to be willing simply to be present with others. Help me to be quiet."

Mrs. Hensley comes in to stand beside Jill's bed, sharing common memories of a distant youth. She leans on a walking cane and speaks warmly, lovingly.

"It don't seem but yesterday we was living neighbors, Jill," she sighs.

"No, it don't," Jill shakes her head in reply. "It's sure good of you to come by, Mattie."

"I got to go now, honey." Mattie reaches over to touch Jill's arm. "Now you just remember, the good Lord loves you. You just pray to him, you hear? He can heal your body. You just trust him and he'll heal you."

"I know it," says Jill, her tired voice hanging on to the thread of hope held out by her friend.

It is early evening, and the small hospital room is spilling over with people. I enter and speak softly to Jill's husband, Ray, saying maybe I should come back another time.

"Now just you come on in here." Jill's deep voice, weak but commanding, fills the room. "I don't want you to leave," she smiles. I smile in return, greet the others, and say, "I won't leave, Jill."

"I want to say good-bye," Jill announces to us. "Now I know this is hard. Hard on my children, especially. But it's got to be done." Her voice softens. "It's not easy to say good-

bye." Jill's daughter, Barbara, is crying. Tears come to all of us. Jill's tone is subdued but sure, her eyes close as she continues.

"I'm getting ready to enter that Golden Circle. Come on in to the Golden Circle. Come in, Barbara. Come in, all my children and grandchildren. Come in, Ray and Lena, and all my friends and neighbors. Come in, all babies and children, all sick people and well people. Come in, old and young, rich and poor, those in their right minds and those demented."

For a moment it is as if Jill were issuing a great heavenly invitation, beckoning us all to come, to enter that place where suffering is no more. It is as if through that weary, simple speech, we hear the very voice of God.

Elaine Stoltzfus
Kentucky

Come to me, all you who are weary and burdened. . . . Take my yoke upon you and learn from me,
for I am gentle and humble in heart, and you will find rest for your souls. Matthew 11:28-29

HOSPITALITY AMIDST ASHES

We were instantly awake as the 105-mm cannons at the airport started their nightly harassment. We listened to the whine of each shell as it arced its deadly trajectory through the night. The earth rumbled as each shell exploded on impact. They sounded uncommonly close—perhaps landing in Nghia Hanh. We thought of friends in the refugee camps there. Whose life would be snuffed out tonight? Whose home destroyed?

In the morning, Earl and I got on the Lambretta and headed the scooter south from the MCC house in the provincial center, asking people as we went where the artillery shells hit. About ten kilometers out of town, we were directed west across the rice paddies toward a large grove of tall bamboos. We turned onto a dirt path between hedges of bright pink bougainvillea and banana trees, greeting villagers on their way to the market or to rice fields. They pointed to an opening in the thick green foliage.

Parking the scooter outside, we entered a clearing where an older couple in their black, peasant pajamas stooped over, picking up pieces of bamboo and tin roofing. What remained of their home and belongings was scattered in splintered fragments around their scorched courtyard.

Seeing us enter, they quickly stood up and came toward us with welcoming smiles. They seemed to know who we were. They had seen us drive in and out of the refugee camp not far away.

Their story of the previous night's events came tumbling out, not in self-pitying tones but with a dignity and defiance that we found common among Quang Ngai peasants.

It was not the first time their house had been destroyed. In fact, this was the fifth time. When they heard the first artillery shell explode nearby, they quickly took refuge in their bunker, a pit dug in the earth beneath their bed. But one of the shells scored a direct hit on their small house. They graciously did not mention that our country had sent these shells. Rather, they drew us in with open hospitality.

As the man related their story, I noticed the woman had moved away and was bent over, in the midst of her total loss, collecting splinters of bamboo and broken tree branches. She put them in a pile as if to start a fire, then stood up and looked at me apologetically.

"I was going to boil tea for you, but I just realize I have no teapot." She moved across the courtyard and picked up the mangled remains of her teakettle.

"Forgive me. Please come again when we have rebuilt our house."

Pat Hostetter Martin
Vietnam

He has sent me . . . to bestow on them a crown of beauty instead of ashes,
the oil of gladness instead of mourning. Isaiah 61:1-4

Blessed
are the meek,
for they will inherit
the earth.

LA VIEJA

I saw her every weekday morning on my daily walk through Cochabamba to the small Protestant school where I taught English to Bolivian teenagers. She sat in a doorsill along Avenida de Flores, her flat calloused feet planted firmly on the sidewalk. She wore a ragged sweater against the early chill of the Andean morning and on very cold days pulled a knitted shawl around her shoulders as well. She was a vendor, her only produce a few overripe bananas scattered in a large basket. The first few times I passed her humble business establishment, we simply glanced at each other, saying nothing. When we realized we were going to be a regular part of each other's mornings, we began exchanging greetings.

"Good morning, senorita."

"Good morning, senora," I replied.

Our conversation never went beyond this greeting. Toward the end of the school year, I spent a week in La Paz. The next Monday as I walked past her, she said, "Good morning, senorita." Then a smile warmed her face, "And welcome back," she added.

There was so much about the old woman, *la vieja,* I did not know. I didn't know how old she was, where she lived, or who her family was. I didn't know a single experience of her past. I didn't even know her name.

She was simply elderly, friendly, and poor. But I sensed that in spite of her simple life, or perhaps because of it, she possessed a great deal of strength and peace.

Today back in North America, my life is crowded with many demands on my time and energy. I am active in our church, my children are young, and I am in the process of establishing a new career. Some days the hassles and problems leave me exhausted and frustrated. But when I find a few moments to be alone, to close my eyes to the immediate surroundings, I often find myself wandering back through the years to Cochabamba, along Avenida de Flores, to the lady who rests on the doorsill and sells bananas. The memories of her fill me with peace and simplicity and remind me of the transience of all things, including frustration and pain. As I approach, she looks up, smiles, and says, "Welcome back."

Rita Smith
Bolivia

Since we are surrounded by such a great cloud of witnesses . . .
let us run with perseverance the race marked out for us. Hebrews 11:39—12:3

ONGOLE GIRL

Long wait on the Ongole Station platform
Alternately standing, sitting, peering
For the late train

A young girl in grimy, gray dress
With disheveled hair
Sits shyly watching us
Then, as if on cue,
She softly asks for money

Do you go to school?
At that her face crumples
She bursts into tears
Where is your mother?
I have no one
Where do you stay?
She gestures toward the station platform
Here

Pained by her tears
We hand her some coins
Her tears stop
She stands up
Thanks us with folded hands
Namastee

We watch her wander off
To sit among the others
Sleeping on the station platform
She examines the coins
Tossing them from hand to hand

Later she again discovers us
Still waiting for our train
She stops
Searching our faces carefully
Slowly a smile crosses her face
Then we are called to platform edge
The arriving train brings movement, action
Our friend
Is lost in the crowd

Rumbling along on the train
From Ongole to Hyderabad
Diwali night
Festival of Lights
Tiny clay lamps
Flicker from windows and doors
Softly lighting the sky

It is a celebration of triumph
Of light over darkness
Of good over evil
Through the light
I still see the young girl's face
We gave so little
She gave so much

She came to us directly
With her humanity
Her pain
In her shy smile
Was an invitation to love
A celebration
Of compassion over guilt

Fern Martin
India

Unless you change and become like children, you will never enter the Kingdom of heaven.
The greatest in the Kingdom of heaven is the one who . . . becomes like this child. Matthew 18:1-6, TEV

A MOMBIN CHRISTMAS STORY

Feeling homesick, we decided to splurge and buy a turkey for Christmas Eve dinner. We radioed some fellow workers in nearby Pignon and asked them to buy us a medium-sized $12 turkey from their local market. A comical set of miscommunications landed us "simple living" Mombin-ites a frozen, U.S. imported, ten-pound genuine Butterball turkey direct from Port-au-Prince, to the tune of $32.50.

The day before Christmas we extricated the turkey with awe and anticipation from its net bag and plastic wrapper. We pored over *The Joy of Cooking* to learn how to roast a turkey. Inexperienced though we were, our cooperative cooking efforts—and pooled "care packages"—produced an indescribable feast: mashed potatoes, filling, gravy, squash, salad, and bread. All could have lived happily ever after (with minor guilt pains and some bloated stomachs) if it had not been for Zina.

Zina was a beggar woman whom we had first met several weeks before Christmas. This desperately crazy, pitiful human being had confounded us all, and we were unable to respond. It was hard to be near her, impossible to talk with her, and yet there she sat in the side yard of the MCC unit house. After a huddled discussion, someone got her a peanut-butter sandwich, which she consumed ravenously, huddled under the protective hood she made with her robe.

Our anguished questions raged both spoken and unspoken: "But what if she gets used to coming here?" "Where is her family?" "Isn't she a community responsibility?" "What caused her to become this way?" "What if she dies?" We all grappled with her, each in our own heart, each in our own way. Over those next few weeks a sweater, some underwear, a sheet, and a new dress adorned her at various times.

The day before Christmas I saw her as I crossed the town square. I hurried along head down, hoping she wouldn't see me and follow. I didn't want anyone to spoil our turkey feast. At the Christmas Eve mass that night, who should come and sit by us but Zina. Oblivious to her rags, she stood up and began to chant and sway in a spontaneous prelude to the otherwise well-planned service.

On her head was the bright orange net from our Swifts Premium Butterball turkey. She had been scavenging in our garbage, no doubt, looking for her Christmas present.

The irony of that moment was so intense—I had to laugh, but might as easily have cried. The relief of my laughter stirred something awake in me. I became aware that God was using Zina to help us understand the essence of Christmas: Jesus is born in our midst again and again, weak and seemingly ridiculous to us proud and confident people who remain again and again confounded.

Mary Ellen Galante
Mombin Crochu, Haiti

God chose the foolish things of the world to shame the wise;
God chose the weak things of the world to shame the strong. 1 Corinthians 1:18-31

A MAN BLACK

My patient is a large black man.
  With broad strong shoulders.
  Could I have bid for him on the block?
    Made him my slave?
  Lashed his body when he didn't please me?

His dark brown eyes rarely engage mine.
  Does he see me as his brother?
    Created in the same God image?

His blood pressure is high.
  Could it be the years of oppression?
    Tension?

His heart beats steadily. It pulses life.
  But his life does not include a family,
    A satisfying job,
A vital place in society.

His joints are misshapen from hard work.
  Work of his choosing?
    Or someone else's?

His bowels rumble noisily.
  Bowels! The depths of a man.
    Where compassion comes from.
  What does he feel deeply?
    What moves him?

His feet. Beautiful feet!
  Let them be free to
    Move where they will,
      Live where they will,
        Rest where they will.

His skin is rich brown.
  It is the major difference between him and me.
    But what a difference!

The black man, my patient, my brother!
  God, why can't we know each other?

Herbert E. Myers, Jr., M.D.
Mississippi

There is neither Jew nor Greek, slave nor free, male nor female,
for you are all one in Christ Jesus. Galatians 3:26—4:7

KALAHARI BUSHMEN

We headed the MCC pickup truck out of the village and into the cold dawn. We shivered as we jounced and rattled over the eight miles of rough sand track and dry riverbeds. Some thirty minutes later, we jolted to a stop in a desolate stretch of stunted thorn trees and dry grass. A blanket of silence settled like dust over the scene.

"Well," Maarten asked, "Do you see the village?" I squinted into the bush, only vaguely seeing traces of hut-like shapes by the way some of the branches were bent. We picked a path through the trees and in a few minutes entered a clearing . . . and another century.

Around a small fire crouched a circle of people, hands outstretched as if to coax some warmth and protection from the morning chill. I waited at the edge of the clearing as Maarten went forward to exchange greetings. I wondered how welcome we would be and tried to be inconspicuous. This proved to be difficult, as a moment later, movement at my feet led me to the discovery that I was standing, uninvited, in someone's bedroom! The "room" consisted of a low tree surrounded by a semicircle of leafy branches stuck in the ground to act as a windbreak. In a hollow in the ground lay a skin mat, a sleeping man, and a blanket.

I was grateful when the "old ones" at the fire broke into toothless smiles and beckoned me to join them. Gingerly I approached, aware now of the many people still asleep around us. Most were waiting for the sun to heat the air before leaving the warmth of their blankets. Some of these were the wood-carvers we had come to see, so we too squatted by the fire, shivered, and watched the stars fade as the sun rose red in the east over Serowe.

A young woman threw some tea leaves and sugar into the large, blackened tin can that served as a kettle, while a boy went off to milk one of the cows they tend for cattle owners. He returned shortly with his USAID vegetable oil tin, "A Gift from the People of America," half full of milk. Two chipped enameled mugs were found and the old ones graciously offered us tea. Clashing thoughts of typhoid fever and formal ladies' teas back home raced through my mind as I glanced at the hot brown water, scooped from a sandy hole in the dry riverbed. They wanted us to feel welcomed. They were offering us their best. We, the guests, drank first, then the cups were rinsed in a tin of water and passed full and steaming to the next two people.

Sitting there we could look out from their

Do not worry about your life. . . . See how the lilies of the field grow. . . .
Will [God] not much more clothe you? Matthew 6:25-30

low hill to the wealthy village of Serowe, where we lived. In another direction, the Masuzulu village was visible with its well-kept houses, prosperous cornfields, and tin-smithing yards. The people around me, by contrast, had nothing. And yet, as I looked around the fire at those peaceful, welcoming faces, it was difficult to say who was really the poorer. I was filled with respect and admiration. They were survivors, truth-knowers. They lived in unity with the earth and maintained a joyful humanness in the midst of abject poverty. Although they had few possessions, they had given me a valuable gift—an opportunity to enjoy simple human companionship, to share the basics of life, to appreciate a sunrise in silence. I encountered genuine hospitality. It was a rare chance to see myself and others as we really are. A chance to look at the world, for a moment, through the eyes of the Creator.

Nancy Snyder Cressman
Botswana

Blessed

are those who
hunger and thirst
for righteousness,
for they will be filled.

GREASED HISTORY

It's almost ten years now.
I know
'cause my baby will be ten years old.
That's a decade
that some are calling
change and progress.
Looks more like
an ant climbing
a greased hula hoop.

My baby was born
the day they signed the contract
and buried Lawrence Jones.

He's the union man
that got shot
for putting nails
in the driveway of a scab—
or so they say.
All depends on who you listen to,
what you end up believing.

Anyway
my baby was born
the day they signed the contract—
born to follow the books
of cooing and crawling.

The men had been on strike
for 13 months before they got the union
at Brookside.
That contract rolled up
health benefits
safety rules
and better pay into one bundle.
But what the miners
really wanted to say
in that 13 months of sitting out
was that
the operators
didn't own them anymore
that things had changed.

Back then,
times were good
for the miners at Brookside,
back
when my baby was learning
to walk and talk
and play ring-around-the-rosy.

And then—
well—
depending on whom you listen to,
some would say
that contract
ripped Brookside out of business.
So that
early in the 80s
when the economy went sour
and people didn't want steel
and the factories didn't need
as much coal—
Brookside got sold
and the men got laid off.
And there they were
sitting around again
for a long time,
thinking about Detroit.

A couple years later
when my baby
was writing her name with loops,
the mine started hiring back—
under new ownership.
And the men
wanted those jobs
bad—
those jobs
with half the pay
and skimpy benefits
and rock falls most every day.

'Cause a man
has to work and have a job
even if it means
someone owns him.
Safety can't afford to be
"the mainest thing" anymore.

So it looks to me
like the hoop's
made about one turn
in these ten years.
My baby rides a bike
and knows her multiplication tables
but it seems to me
that things get divided up
around here
pretty much like they did
a decade ago.
Back then
this county
didn't have fast food
or K Mart.
But I reckon
about the same people
have the money to spend now
as then.
So what's ten years
more or less
when the outcome is the same—
just different owners?

What does the Lord require of you? To act justly and to love mercy
and to walk humbly with your God. Micah 6:1-8

And who am I
to stand in the way
of these forces
that have been set in motion,
that will have their way?
Who am I
to stand
like a rock
in front of a tire?

I am
at once
no one
and someone.
I am no one
'cause I can't fight
power with power,
both for lack of strength
and lack of philosophy.
But I am
someone
because I have the will
to stay
and make the hoop
a bit less slippery.

Besides,
my baby
is watching.

Evie Yoder Miller
Kentucky

DANCE IN THE DANGER

I took a plane from Manila to Negros in the middle of the night.
I was trying to save money.
When I got to the bus station at 5:00 a.m.
I discovered the bus to Cebu wouldn't leave until noon.
I chewed myself out for scrimping on airfare
and went to find a cup of coffee.

Noon came and I jumped on the air-con bus to the coast.
We rolled past thousands of acres of sugarcane fields and shacks.
How odd to feel the stream of cool air
while the people we passed burned in the midday heat.
At least they couldn't see me staring at them
through the tinted glass.

We arrived at the dock where our bus would board the ferry.
I decided to wait in the bus until the ferry came
rather than face the stares of people in this broken-down port town.
A girl of about seven boarded the bus with a tray of candy.
She came to my seat.

"Candy?"
"No, thank you."
She looked at me.
"Come on, buy some candy."
"No, I don't want any."

She plopped down on the seat beside me.
"You know, my classes end next week and
I have to pay my teacher 17 pesos if I want to graduate."
A mere eighty cents, I thought.
"Can't your father pay?"
"No, he used to work in the cane fields,
but now he has no job."

"Where do you live?"

"Outside Escalante."

My heart stopped. Escalante.

That's the town where not long ago twenty-seven farmers

were shot down during a peaceful march for food.

This is a child of Escalante.

She was talking.

"I bring the money I made to my family."

"You have no money for school then?"

"I could pay, but then, what would we eat?"

"That is hard."

She got up and tried to sell to the sleepy man in the next row.

"Wait," I said, "what's your name?"

"Angie."

"Angie, I think I need some candy after all."

She smiled.

"How much?"

"Well, I'm going to a big meeting. Maybe fifteen pesos worth."

Her nimble fingers fluttered through the candy.

"Let's pick out all the good ones.

"These butterballs are my favorite, but those are good too."

She scrounged a used plastic bag for the candy

and skipped off the bus.

"Thank you, Patricia. Thank you. Thank you."

I felt good, yet somehow disturbed that I should

have the power to make this child so happy—or unhappy.

I got off the bus and sat down on a rock along the shore.

I combed my hand absently through the sand.

Angie saw me and slid up beside me.

"Do you like shells?"

"Yes, I do."

"Look, here is a nice one."

"Oh, yes, that is nice."

"Take it."

She spied another shell.

"Here, this is pretty."

Angie's friends gathered and all began to bring me shells.

"Do you like this one?"

More children dropped their baskets to join the search.

"Look, isn't this one pretty, Patricia? It's for you."

Shells overflowed from my hands into my lap.

Bits of blue and pink and green and glistening white.

Broken and whole, delicate and crusted.

Then I saw Angie look at her best friend, who nodded.

Angie pulled something off her finger.

"Here, this is for you."

A small black plastic ring with gold lettering on the front:

"DANCE," it said.

"Angie, I cannot take your ring."

"No, it is for you." She was sure.

I slipped it on my smallest finger.

"I will not take this off. Thank you, Angie.

Thank you. Thank you."

I took her hand.

A horn blew. The ferry had arrived.
The children helped me gather up my things and I boarded the bus.
I looked out the window.
Angie was trying to wave, but she couldn't see me for the tint.
I waved.
She saw the movement, grinned, and waved back furiously.
The bus pulled onto the ferry
and we couldn't see each other anymore.

I stared at the ring.
Did it say "dance" or "danger"?
It looked like "dange." Perhaps the *r* had rubbed off.
Or was it just a funny looking *c*?
I was struck with the paradox:
Danger and dance.

Certainly, Angie, a child from this place of danger, was dancing.
She had pulled me out of my stuffy comfort
and had invited me
to the hot and joyous dance of a struggling people.

Perhaps to struggle is to dance in the danger.
To resist those that would tie your hands and bind your feet,
that would cut you off
from the rhythms of the earth and human history.

From inside the bus you think you could never join the dance.
But when you step off, you realize that something has changed.
You feel the wind, the warm earth.
You begin to feel the rumblings of the feet of the people
and you begin to move, one step at a time.

At first, you follow the dance of those around you,
but you can't quite mimic their steps.
If you stay with them, you gradually
begin to sense the next step, and the next.
One step flows from the other.
You learn and move and learn as you move.

You begin to know that this is the dance you were called to do.
This is the dance of your life.

Patricia Wagner
*Philippine*s

You have changed my sadness into a joyful dance; you have taken away my sorrow
and surrounded me with joy. Psalm 30:1-12, TEV

THE BAPTIST LIKED LOCUSTS

Almost all the letters our family has received recently have expressed admiration for the sacrifices we have made by leaving the comforts of North America for the rigors of the Third World. I have trouble accepting that admiration because I am not sure whether I have sacrificed anything.

I love rice with bean sauce and grilled pork without fat. I can think of nothing better than sitting down to eat a half dozen tree-ripened oranges or an avocado smeared on fresh bread.

In Haiti I have time to reflect deeply on the Bible in today's world. Why do the prophets talk about widows and orphans? What does it mean to love your enemies when those same enemies have been systematically destroying the land and livelihood of your peasant friends? In North America I have to pay good money to go to conferences to hear people talk about these biblical questions which I now reflect on every day.

I'll bet John the Baptist felt the same way. I am sure his family and friends kept bugging him to lead a normal life, move back to town, perhaps take up a trade like his cousin, Jesus. I'll bet he told them that he preferred the time to think and reflect and pray. I'll bet he even told them that he liked locusts and wild honey.

Ham Brown
Haiti

Prepare the way for the Lord, make straight paths for him. Matthew 3:1-12

NU COTZ'IJ

Let me say that the yellow Datsun pickup
   is part of this.
Without it we could not have come to this village.
Nor could we have bumped the view
   into different pictures:
Of boulders and dry riverbeds
Of patterned fields on steep mountain slopes
   Of burned-out villages
Of the father, caught in my rearview mirror,
   hunched over his small daughter with a broken back,
   packed in gypsum dressing.

The Datsun is full.
Driver, passengers, and car are one.
We are dirty and tired.
At the inn in Nebaj we meet
   the local telegraphist
   together with the schoolteacher.
They take turns at the inn's only faucet
   in the center of the yard
   and comment on their beds.
One is too soft and one a bit too hard.

Thoughts about my pregnant wife
   and our small son
   a day's journey away
Are invisible wires
Which bring them together with us
   in this place.

How to capture the unusual beauty of this place
   the Maya-Quiche area
   of northern Guatemala

Sometimes I sit and sketch
I have no camera
A camera eliminates the factor of time.
The quality of an experience of beauty
   said my architecture teacher
Is related to the time factor.

I smile
The quality of this experience relates to what happened
   earlier this day
Not only to the quality of the inn beds
And the lone water spigot in the empty yard
   scratched by chickens.

I remember the women in Sacatepequez
   though I think of them in other colors
Who pass my workshop everyday
With big water jars on their heads.

One should take a picture of them
   and print it seven times
Then hang all seven in a line.
For every morning they pass
   seven times
Until they have enough.
In the evening again.

The fullness of color
   the abundance of form!
It is here and there
   in their embroidery
   in the bodies graceful even with age

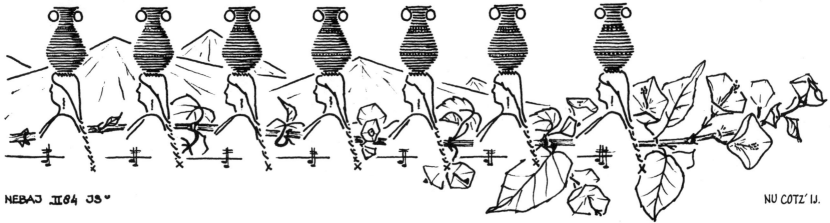

NEBAJ II84 JS

NU COTZ'IJ.

In the tiny irregular fields flung like pebbles
   in patterns across the mountain slope.
Abundancy of scale
   human figures and
The sharp-shadowed openings
   in the thick white-plastered adobe walls.

The pictures of my architecture teacher
         showed
      fine samples of nerves
      or veins in leaves
      and exact crystalline structures
Pictures of tree rows
   cultivated to enrich the structures and
   the natural rhythms of life.
There is structure in creation.
An architect
   my teacher said
Should create in harmony with the
      environment.

The tiny girl in gypsum
   with the broken back
And her father
They are part of the structure.
I must try to blend into their rhythms
   forms, shapes, colors.

This trip earned the name
   nu cotz'ij.*
Yes, I keep seeing "my flower"
   over and over.
The beauty is nontransferable.
If I tell this story to a friend
   will he feel the bumpy road?
When I go home
Can I carry some of the flower's beauty
      over the mountains?
What else can I give the war victims
      and widows
The men whose daughters die
   of broken backs?

*Kachchiquel flower

Even the night does not take away my
      thoughts
   the bed is much too soft
We rise at dawn to leave
   it is chilly.

The countryside and roads
   are lost in thick fog
When it lifts, there will be signs
   of war and violence.
I will see charcoaled skeletons of houses
   floundering for new rhythms
Tiny new flowers coming up
   in destroyed dwellings.

I am like the fog
   I feel the tender flowers
   pushing at my stomach.

Jacobo Shiere
Guatemala

The desert and the parched land will be glad; the wilderness will rejoice and blossom.
Like the crocus, it will burst into bloom; it will rejoice greatly and shout for joy. Isaiah 35:1-2

Blessed
are the merciful,
for they will be shown
mercy.

THE OGRE'S PRAYER FOR CHILDREN

God bless them
God bless the dear little children
With foul mouths
My anger
Only a spark—ebbs
How can I be angry

I smile
As they run
From the Ogre
God bless them
God bless the dear little children
Take the mangoes
Leave the lemons
There for me
The Ogre

God bless them
God bless the dear little children
With thieves' fingers
Bless them anyway
Protect them
From the Ogre.

Linda EppHeise
India

Let the children come to me . . . for of such is the kingdom. Matthew 19:13-22, NIV/KJV

THE RAIN AND JUSTICE

It is a cold rainy night.
I sit comfortably in my cozy house
music pouring out of the stereo
a glass of Singha in my hands.
I am with friends.
I am happy.
Our talk is of an intellectual nature—
of how we will build a better world
of what is wrong with capitalism and
                    communism
and what kind of ism we will create.

Outside an old woman sits
protected from the rain by cardboard
humming a quiet song
which we hear when our stereo is quiet.
We are accustomed to her presence.
She is one of at least a million in the city.
We see something beautiful in her simple life
and her simple expectations.
Even though she is old
she still works hard every day
and seems content with the little she has.
"That is a beautiful life," we say,
as we nurse our drinks,
listen to our stereo
and sit comfortably in our cozy house.

Suddenly her humming turns to angry shouts.
We rush out to see.
Someone wants her to move her cardboard
so he can park his new BMW.
She won't go!
We stand with her.
There is more shouting!
There is anger!
The old lady is strong.
She won't give up her small space
and her cardboard shelter.

Finally the BMW owner tires.
If she will move her shanty
a few meters down the path
he will replace her cardboard
with plywood.
Then he can park his BMW
and her house will be stronger.

We all rejoice!
Justice has been achieved!

The old woman squats under her plywood
and hums her song again
in rhythm with the falling rain.
Once again we return to our cozy house
our Singha
our stereo
and to the new ism we will create.

And only the rain is outraged
by this concept of justice.

Max Ediger
Thailand

*They trample on the heads of the poor as upon the dust of the ground
and deny justice to the oppressed.* Amos 2:6-16

CANDEIAS CHALICE

There is little of anything in Candeias.
The paved road ends and the dirt road begins.
The salt is sweet and pungent drifting in on the ocean breezes.
The waves of high tide are audible from the road
just a stone's throw away.

At that last bus stop the countryside is all sand—dirty sand.
Frolicking goat kids nibble dry stubs of burnt vegetation,
while dirty human kids play with old cans and cardboard between
square little woodplank houses, dark and dank.
A heavy, ill air bears up the smell from a pigsty nearby.
The orphanage rises incongruously out of the sandy flatland,
and is surrounded on all sides by the tiny shacks.

When I arrived that day, I met Joyce, the orphanage housemother, leaving,
the gate left open behind her, as she hurried out.
She explained that a young girl in one of those outlying hovels
had been stricken with fever two weeks ago and was not improving.
I remembered that night just two weeks earlier
when the northeast Brazilian sky tore open in cloudburst.
Swift arrows had lashed suddenly from the Southern Cross
to that little shanty in Candeias.
April lightning had smitten the earth,
and a small girl with flowing hair and large, inquiring eyes
was seized in a heat that some called typhus, others malaria,
and all feared to be meningitis.

The only "medicines" available in Candeias come in cans.
Joyce was carrying two in her hand as we arrived at the plank hut.
I watched as the two cans, the future chalices of the trash pile,
were extended as a sacred offering.
"Orangeade," they read.

Long after they have been opened, discarded, then rusted,
the children play with the cans.
The crusty, eroded metal revolves through all of its cyclical
                    functions.
When it has spent its share of seasons,
rainy, then dry, then rainy again,
amidst the plastic bags and pieces of cardboard,
old tires and split coconut shells,
the litany of recycle is pronounced by the children.
Seated in the brown infected sand, their hands are wondrous,
their minds inventive as the cans are thrown into a million dreams.

First the cans become fancy cars, then tunnels for the cars;
now, one upon another they are towers and lofty castle turrets, or
apartment skyscrapers there in the distance against the horizon,
where their mothers work as maids, feeding the babies of the rich.
The dream machines within their heads are
whirring, spinning, frightening, delighting, traveling, returning.
Those rusty cans, former vessels of the salvation of children,
are the vehicles.
Their little discolored hands are sanctified in their art,
as the hands of the painter, the sculptor, the engraver, the priest.
The can is a vessel, a lovely golden chalice,
studded with jewels that glimmer and sparkle like ocean pebbles.
The sacrifice is offered again, as another can is unearthed,
with far prettier gems, they say.
See how it glitters! How magnificently set are the precious stones.
Surely this chalice must have been grasped by many a royal hand.

Suddenly like April lightning, the children—
not expecting their toys to turn on them,
having forgotten the ragged edge of the tin so cunningly
                    bejeweled—
watch with new wonder as bright red, living blood
pours over that rusty edge of diamonds, sapphires, and topaz.
A Candeias chalice.

Tom Capuano
Brazil

*We have this treasure [of God's light] in earthen vessels, to show that this all-surpassing power
is from God and not from us.* 2 Corinthians 4:1-12, KJV/NIV

Blessed

are the pure in heart,
for they will see God.

ON HOLY GROUND

A bar in Olongapo
A bar full of sailors
And prostitutes
Drinking, laughing, yelling.
Holy Ground?
Moses took off his shoes
When he stood on Holy Ground.

I didn't take off my shoes in the bar
But the space we created
Susan and I
Amid the raucousness of sailors on liberty
Became Holy Space to me.

When I walked into the bar that evening
I was exhausted
With little energy to talk to Susan.
She is such an intense person
Struggles deeply with depression
Has tried to take her life.
She showed me the scars on her wrists.

We talked about her hurts
Her inability to trust the sailors
Since the father of her baby
Abandoned them both.

"They are playing with me.
I don't want to play.
I want someone to love me
And my daughter, P. J.
I don't need much money

Just enough for my needs
And some love."

We talked about God.
Susan wonders why
God gives her so many trials.
She says to God,
"You send me trials.
Why don't you help me?"
Like Job
Susan has the courage to question God,
Such courage must be rooted deeply in faith.

"God wants me to be strong
To keep trying.
I will not give up.
I cannot take my life
Because of P. J.
But my body is tired
My mind confused.
I want to help P. J.
But I can't even pay my rent.
Why does God send me these trials?"

We talked about spirituality
What does it mean?
We talked about what is inside a person
About our relationship to God.
We agreed
It's not dependent on
What a person does
But on who she is.
Susan seemed to understand.

"Do you believe you are a good person?"
She was not sure.
Said she sometimes lies to sailors
To get more money to pay rent
And buy food.
Said she is sometimes angry.
I thought
Thank God you are angry.

Our worlds may be different
Our theology words may be different
But would I have her courage to
Keep on living
Keep on praying
Keep on challenging God?

The jukebox was playing loudly
Women were serving drinks
Sailors were getting drunk.
Susan and I sat talking
From the deep places of
Our hearts and souls.

Spirit God
God Love
Was there with us
Our small corner was Holy Space.

Brenda Stoltzfus
Philippines

"Do not come any closer," God said. "Take off your sandals,
for the place where you are standing is holy ground." Exodus 3:1-5

PARKING LOT THEOLOGY

I am going to an evening soccer game with a friend.
It is Ramadan, the month in which devout Muslims
abstain from all food and drink during daylight hours
in commemoration of Allah's revealing the Qur'an to Muhammad.

"How did you spend the day?" I ask.
"I did a lot of praying," he replies, then adds reflectively,
"I hope God hears my prayers."
My mind searches for a response:
    —Oh, I'm sure he did!
    —Of course he can't—you're pagan.
    —Why pray more now than at other times?
    —What interesting customs you Muslims have.

I muse silently as we walk and then venture,
"If your heart is right, then God will hear your prayers."
Do I really believe this?
Not quite the way I've stated it.
I need to qualify my comment.
Memories of lectures I've given on prayer crowd through my mind,
theological distinctions, fine points by Ellul, Hallesby, and Buttrick—
but how does one communicate all this
while walking through a parking lot to a stadium?

A long silence. Then he responds.
"That's what we believe, too.
I am seeing more and more the many points of our religions
where we have similar ideas."
Now what? My reply could be:
    —Oh no, our religions are quite different. After all, you reject
        Jesus' divinity.
    —Oh yes, they are really just different ways of saying the same
        things.
    —The government doesn't want me discussing religions. I can't
        talk further.

There isn't time to formulate all the theological niceties.
Instead, we begin to talk about our concepts of God and his
        authority,
what we understand about him and his relationship to the world.
We make significant self-disclosures, involving psychological risk.
And then we enjoy the soccer game.
Theology in a parking lot.
A beginning.

Vern Ratzlaff
Egypt

*The Spirit helps us in our weakness. We do not know what we ought to pray,
but the Spirit . . . intercedes for us with groans that words cannot express.* Romans 8:18-27

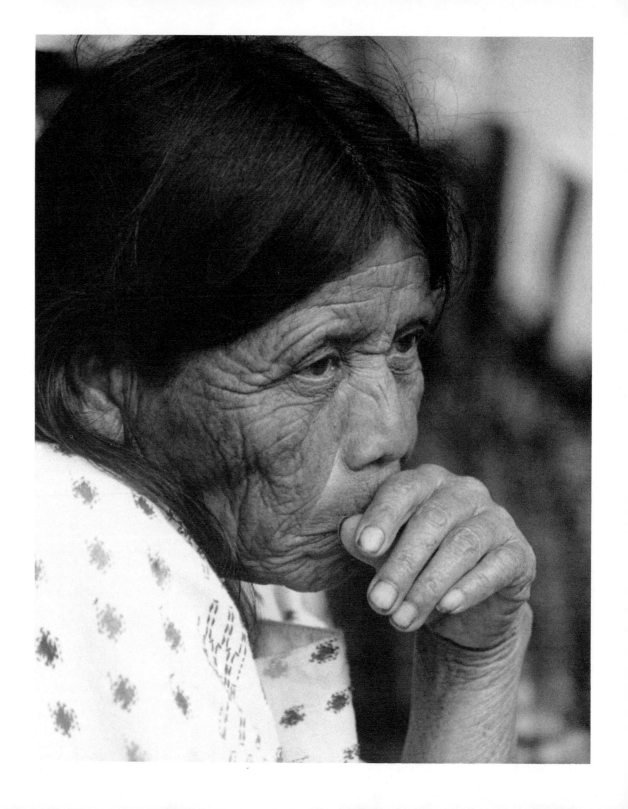

HELENA'S STORY

It was at a consultation in Paraguay
Helena Oliver told her story
Helena was a social worker sent by the government of Argentina
To work with the Mataca Indian people
After working with them for a while
She was converted to the Christian faith

Now she was to give an address
On the ethics of development

Helena began
  You asked me to report on the Matacas
  The Matacas are my friends
  It is hard to speak analytically
  About those close to you

  I used to ask them
  What do you live on
  They answered
    The trees
    The rivers
    When we fish and hunt
    It is not work
    It is our life

  I asked
  About the land
  Whose lands are these
  They answered
    The land is the Lord's
    Our place is the house of God
    All things have life
    But things are not gods

Anthropologists call us polytheists
But they do not understand

The way we live with one another and
The way we relate to God
Is what we understand

White people have made the law
We don't understand it
But we have to follow it
The government asks us
Do you want a health center
We say yes
Do you want a tractor
We say yes

But after a while the tractor breaks down
And everyone laughs
To live and eat while maintaining a tractor is hard
The Mataca cannot laugh under the heavy weight of a tractor

We give them material goods to solve their problems
But all they ask is that we live with them
And believe in them

To establish mutual confidence
We must not think of them as they
And of us as we
Are we not made of the same clay
The project is unimportant
Apart from our relationships with people

The Mataca taught me
They understood me
They talked to me about faith
They never tried to make me like they are
They responded to me
They didn't let me down
The Mataca theology was not so clearly defined
But it touched me

So where does this leave us
What is our ethic
Our ethic is embedded in our relationships
In our attitudes

We so easily trust in things
Matacas trust in God
And therefore can more easily
Live like birds of the air
And flowers of the field

The Mataca word for God means
The one who doesn't know how to die

The consultation came to an end
But Helena's words linger
As I ponder the purifying impact
Of Mataca faith shared

Menno Wiebe
Canada

Seek ye first the kingdom of God, and his righteousness;
and all these things shall be added unto you. Matthew 6:31-34, KJV

A CUCKOO

If I had not awakened,
I could not hear or know
the grace of God.

A MOMENTARY BEAUTY

Let us gaze
at things quickly disappearing . . .

icicles hanging from the eaves . . .
the work of God. . . .

INTENTLY

I gaze
at a red dragonfly
swallowed into the blue sky.

I listen
to the weakening voices of insects
in the sound of rain.

I quiet my heart and
search for the will of God
in morning prayer.

A GUEST

This morning after the violent wind,
the garden is carpeted with fallen leaves. . . .
Who is the guest?

Ah, it's you, Jesus,
who became poor for me.

Can I give some persimmons?
Would you like some walnuts?

SNOWY ROAD

Lord,
you must have been cold
walking on the snowy road.

Please help yourself to
some red-bean soup with rice cakes
my sister-in-law made.

Make yourself warm.
My heart is warm
just being with you.

MEMORY

The vines of the morning glories
which have bloomed every morning. . . .

The autumn wind swings them,
as if talking, and remembers word after word. . . .

My heart which has been quiet
trembles faintly, too.

TANKA

My ears left
unparalyzed,
hear the sound
of icicles
falling from the eaves.

AMONG THOSE

I am among those
whom Jesus
watches with love,
approaches, speaks to,
and stretches his hands to.

Genzo Mizuno
Japan

Genzo Mizuno died in 1984 at the age of forty-seven. When he was in the fourth grade, he was attacked by brain paralysis. Since then, he was unable to move his hands or legs. He could not speak. He could move only his eyes. He had been sick in bed for thirty-eight years.

When writing his poems, he looked at the chart of Japanese alphabet on the wall and focused on particular letters. His mother followed his eyes, identified the letters, and wrote them down. When she died, his sister-in-law helped him. In this way, he wrote down many poems which we published in four books.

Christ is the center of these poems. They are full of joy and beauty. As we read his poems, which are short with simple diction, we are also filled with celebration because with him we find Christ in every place.

Yorifumi Yaguchi
Japan

Were not our hearts burning within us while he talked with us on the road? Luke 24:13-35

Blessed

are the peacemakers,
for they will be called
children of God.

TO LAY DOWN ONE'S LIFE

Rumbek Secondary School is located 270 miles northwest of Juba in southern Sudan. It was never a stable place, at least not after the long civil war. Students came from many parts of the southern region. The tribal mixture created tensions. Even within the Dinka tribe, clan rivalries often surfaced.

During my first three months of teaching, tensions were running high. Rumbek was parched, January being the middle of the dry season. Students had to line up to use the few faucets available near the dorms. Two Dinka students from rival clans—the Yirol and the Gogrial—had a fight one evening over who was to brush his teeth first. It was quickly broken up by a fellow teacher, but the tension remained. The headmaster, a Yirol, unfairly punished the boy of the Gogrial clan. This irritated Mathon, a teacher from Gogrial, who started to antagonize the Yirols.

The next week I was teaching a chemistry class to second-year students. While I had my back turned, writing something on the board, the class started running outside. I grabbed one of the students before he escaped and asked what was going on. "A fight," he said, "the Dinka students are fighting one another!" Being curious, and somewhat mystified, I joined the rush. Most of the students stopped at the edge of the building. Thinking it was a small fight somewhere, I kept going. A slight mistake. To my left a group of eighty boys gathered, moving toward me, carrying sticks and rocks. Coming from the right an equal-sized, equally armed group was running. After seeing the first rock fly, I made a hasty retreat.

There was little that could be done. The fight seemed beyond stopping by means we teachers had. We all, both Sudanese and expatriate, fled to the safety of our respective homes; all, that is, except for Pastor Reuben Makoi.

Pastor Reuben led the Episcopal church in Rumbek. He taught at the secondary school and acted as an adviser to the Christian students. He was at the school when the riot began. Understanding clan rivalries, though not a Dinka himself, Pastor Reuben quickly went to Mathon's house. A group of students from Yirol was approaching, and Mathon cursed them from his porch as they came. Pastor Reuben forced Mathon inside his house, then went and stood at the gate. The students were angry. They wanted to kill Mathon, who had provoked the riot by stirring up the Gogrial students. Reuben did not move. To kill Mathon, he stated, the students would have to kill him first. One of the Yirols threatened the pastor with a knife. All the while Mathon was yelling abuse at the students through a window.

Pastor Reuben stood at the gate for forty-five minutes until the army arrived. They arrested the Yirols, which by this time included more than students, and placed Mathon in protective custody. Eventually he was sent to Juba on permanent transfer. Reuben's action, risking his own life, probably prevented Mathon's death and the deaths of many others. He never claimed any credit for his action.

What makes a person prepared to lay down his life, even for the life of an enemy?

Wayne Teel
Sudan

It is a difficult thing for someone to die for a righteous person. . . . But God has shown us how much he loves us—it was while we were still sinners that Christ died for us! Romans 5:1-8, TEV

PILGRIMS FOR PEACE

The bells call us to prepare, in the dim grayness before dawn.
Mothers carrying wee ones at breast; running saucy boys.
Old women with bare feet have walked pilgrimages before.
A few men—campesinos who belong to the land.
Girls in bright dresses and rubber sandals;
Called together in the advent of the New Year
When the need for peace urgently requires all.
All of us—male and female, strong and weak, rich and poor—
Must pray for peace in this world.
Peace in this zone, these towns.
Peace between us.
Peace within us.
Everyone is called to this pilgrimage.
I look around at those who gather.
Most are women, the poor, the young, the weak.
God's people answer the call.

A painted wooden cross goes before us.
We walk past white village church and military command post.
Down a dusty road.
To pray for peace we walk into the rising sun.
Like many fibers twisted into string,
We are joined by pilgrims from other villages.
Knit together on one road through the steep hills.
Like twine, together we are stronger.

A chord struck on hand-made guitar
Begins the song that leads us to the plaza,
To the celebration under the sky, in front of many eyes.
They are brave, these who read from the Word of God,
These who denounce the beatings in the presence of those who laid
    the blows.

With courage they call for repentance
That we might seek peace together.

The petitions are real in this corner of Honduras:
We suffer. Be present with us.
    Lord we pray. Hear us. Have mercy.
Speed the tiny light in me to carry hope to one who is despairing.
    Lord we pray. Hear us. Have mercy.
Purge us of harbored hate.
Fill us that we may live rightly with those who have wronged us.
    Lord we pray. Hear us. Have mercy.
Give us strength so that peace can flow from our lives.
    Lord we pray. Hear us. Have mercy.

The words ring so clearly from the wrinkled grandmother
whose knees bend in the gravel next to mine.
    Lamb of God who takes away the sins of the world, grant us peace.
Somehow I know: the Lamb will have mercy.
Can God ignore this grandmother's cry?
Or the risky words of the priest and lay leaders?
Or the feet that have walked in order to pray?

Blessed. We walked the dusty road home
To make our lives prayers of peace.
May it be so.
    Lord we pray.
    Hear us.
    Have mercy.

Carol Rose
Honduras

Love and faithfulness will meet; righteousness and peace will embrace. Psalm 85, TEV

SAND CASTLES

The Lao New Year is a celebration which delights in the cleansing, life-giving power of water. To the uninitiated, it can be rather startling to watch a whole society engage in a three-day romp in the streets, clutching buckets, dippers, and bamboo water guns. Having lived here for four seasons, however, we look forward to this splash of fun under the hot April sun. What could be more fun than dousing an unsuspecting friend or, better yet, total stranger, with a bucketful of water? A great way to beat the heat, these "showers of blessing" also contain lessons in simplicity and exuberance . . . but I am getting ahead of my story.

Lao New Year festivities have their roots in a rather gruesome tale from the world of the gods. It seems there was once an angel who lost a bet in a battle of wits with a very wise man. In accordance with the rules of the bet, the angel was beheaded. In order to prevent fire, drought, or pestilence on the earth, the angel's seven daughters were instructed to pour water on the angel's head once a year. This would guarantee prosperity and fertility. From this arose the tradition of wishing each other well by pouring water at the New Year. Incorporated into religious ceremony, the pouring of water on one another in more ritualistic style signifies the washing away of sins and forgiveness . . . a symbolism strikingly close to baptism.

Luang Prabang is situated along the Mekong River in Laos. On the first day of the New Year, I joined the local Ag Committee, along with hundreds of others, in a dash across the Mekong in long, narrow boats. Armed with buckets, shovels, and a couple of slender, bamboo frames, we were on our way to build a giant sand castle. These castles are built by groups of people along the sandy edge of an island in the Mekong. Some see it as a way of gaining merit from Lord Buddha.

From the moment we stepped into the boat, the celebration began. Several men grabbed the oars and slapped the water with gusto to ensure we didn't arrive dry on the other side. This was further ensured by "greeters" who stood knee-deep in the water as our boat pulled up to the island. Cupping their hands, they splashed us liberally as we all laughed and thanked them profusely.

Dozens of groups had already staked out spots along the sandy island bank to build sand castles. General revelry bubbled around us. In this throng of people, when friend met friend, the result was always the same. After some good-natured joking and backslapping, one would sense the advantage, seize the other by the arm, dash down the gently sloping bank, and fling his wide-eyed friend into the Mekong. This was the happy lot of hundreds of people on that day . . . no one escaped, or particularly cared to.

Amidst all this hubbub we did indeed set about the task of building a sand castle. It ended up being a larger undertaking than I had anticipated, as a great deal of sand and water were required. As the castle began to take shape, some of us got down on our hands and knees and began patting the sand so it would pack and remain firm. This proved to be a temptation too great for the sand shovelers and water flingers. By making only a slight miscalculation, someone at the river's edge could heave water just over the top of the castle and onto our heads. This kept us cool, of course, and the flying sand, which invariably got stuck between our teeth, gave us something to chew on.

While on my knees patting sand, I chanced to work beside Mr. Xieng Pheng, an Ag official from Oudomsai Province. An old Pathet Lao soldier, this man had seen lots of action during the Vietnam War. He had made numerous trips down the Ho Chi Minh trail. Stocky, muscular, and full of life, he was obviously enjoying himself on this afternoon. Despite the frequent showers of water from the buckets of our frolicking friends along the river, we were serious about our sand patting. At least our side of the castle would be firm!

In the middle of patting, chewing sand, and general mayhem, Mr. Pheng stopped, looked at me, and said with a big grin, "My, but we are going to a lot of trouble for the Buddha, aren't we?" I roared with laughter. The longer I thought about it, the more I wondered how this Mennonite boy from the hills of Grantsville, Maryland, ever ended up beside this old Pathet Lao soldier in Communist Laos, building sand castles for a Buddhist celebration! Some moments in life are too remarkable to be explained.

It is redundant, I guess, to say that these people are just like anyone else . . . and we don't often have opportunity to see each other like this. With all our guns, missiles, and bombs, the world is much too threatening a place for friendships. Masks are worn and labels—"communist" or "imperialist"—are fixed on one another. The enemy must remain faceless so that wars can be fought. This way, the Phengs and the Souvandys, the Tituses and the Lindas, can be killed as "guerrilla" or "enemy" without thinking about all the fun we could have had pouring water on each other at New Year's and building castles together in the sand.

Titus Peachey
Laos

When you please the Lord, you can make your enemies into friends. Proverbs 16:1-9, TEV

Blessed

are those who are persecuted
because of righteousness,
for theirs is the
kingdom of heaven.

A BARRIO NATIVITY

In those days there went out a decree from the military governor that all the farmers in the scattered villages of Davao Norte province should abandon their farmsteads and go into the distant headquarters to register. Every farmer was ordered to dismantle his house sufficiently so that the passing military patrols could see through the house without entering, for they suspected the presence of antigovernment rebels in the area. So all the poor farmers of the region tore the siding from their houses and gathered together small bundles of their earthly possessions that they could carry.

And Pasar also went from his village into the town of Laac in the province of Davao Norte. He went there to register with Anita, his wife, who was great with child.

Pasar and Anita took also with them their water buffalo, the family beast of burden. But it was too uncomfortable for Anita to be juggled on the back of the docile beast, so she alighted and walked the five miles to Laac. When they arrived in the town, there were also from the scattered villages great crowds of farmers numbering 12,000 souls, for they had come under orders to register their allegiance to the ruler in Manila.

Lo, there were no hotels or inns in the town of Laac, so the villagers had to find shelter in schoolhouses or under trees for many days, leaving many old people and children sick with pneumonia.

And while they were there the time came for Anita to deliver. There was found a small room behind the town chapel where she gave birth to a newborn son. Anita and Pasar were filled with great joy. They took a part of the name of Anita and part of the name Pasar and named the child: Anisar!

And they took Anisar, the baby, and dedicated him to the Lord.

Earl Martin
Philippines

While they were there, the time came for the baby to be born. Luke 2:1-7

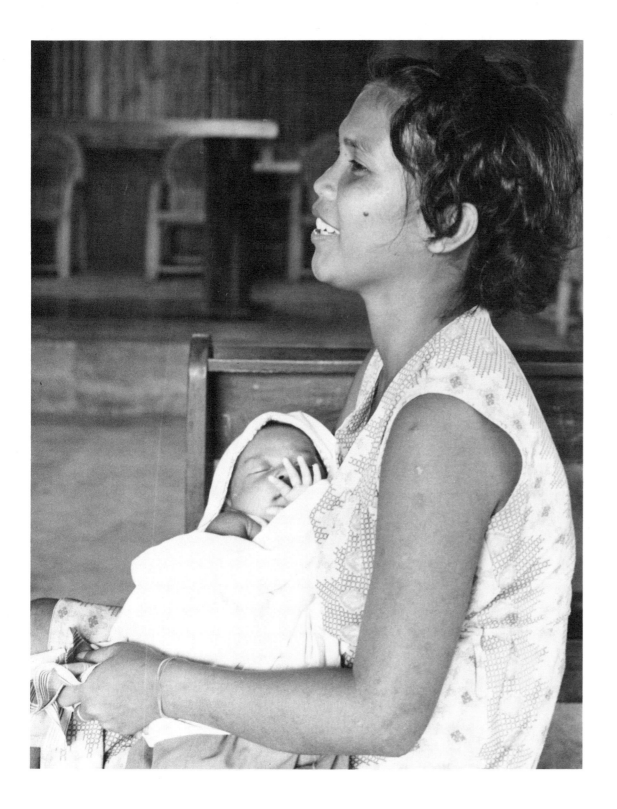

GOOD FRIDAY, 1987

a man holds
the head
of another man
he's just killed
moves in front of the cross
hiding it
and the One on it
from view

a radio man
announces
his latest list
of communists
mingles his voice
with the cry from the cross
till the words
become one

boy soldiers carry
guns
march between
the people kneeling
and the Stations of the Cross
hiding the One
who suffers with them
from sight

a young man
sleeps on a picket line
a bullet enters his head
his mother
and the one at the cross ask
is my son not good
why do they kill him

anger grows to
hatred
threatens
to make me one of them
but hasn't yet taken
the life of
the One on the cross
from mine

Jan Lugibihl
Philippines

*You will listen, O Lord, to the prayers of the lowly; you will give them courage. You will hear
the cries of the oppressed and the orphans; you will judge in their favor,
so that mortal men may cause terror no more. Psalm 10:17-18, TEV*

REDEMPTION

I raced to get to the Christian Building by 10:00 a.m., only to discover that the prayer meeting was beginning "on Korean time," fifteen minutes later than scheduled. The small room was packed. Ham Suk Han, the white-haired "Mahatma Ghandi of Korea," looking as majestic as he is wise, sat among a dozen or so rather well-dressed mothers and wives of imprisoned Christians. I stood alongside several plainly dressed women with ruddy complexions. A missionary explained that they were wives of alleged "communists," six of whom had been sentenced to death. None of the women were Christian, yet they came because the community shared their pain and struggle.

Yun, a Presbyterian minister, stood up to announce that the meeting was about to begin but that first he wanted to advise the participants: "For my prayer last week, I was harshly interrogated by the [Korean] CIA. If anyone here is not willing to risk similar treatment, perhaps he or she should leave now." No one among the forty present moved, so the service began.

I missed at least 80 percent of what was being said, but was gripped by the profound depths of emotion in the prayers. Most of them concerned the some 200 persons imprisoned this year for their political, religious, and social concerns. Coming from Japan, I tried hard to fight back my tears—and not to blow my nose in public!—until I noticed that nearly everyone else in the room was weeping. A wave of inspiration—of judgment and redemption—swept through my body. I was no longer an American, from Japan, passing through Korea. I prayed like I haven't prayed in years. The prisoners' bondage, and their families' suffering, became mine—became ours—in a prayer of confession that rose from our collective souls.

However, I should not imply that my encrusted soul took flight in some ecstasy-fantasy. What happened to all of us that morning was very earthbound: a physical and spiritual rising, standing up to say, "Yes, Lord, we rise to your occasions with our feet firmly planted. Despite our fear we know your purposes."

Jim Stentzel
Korea

So do not fear, for I am with you; do not be dismayed, for I am your God. Isaiah 41:8-10

THE EDITORS

Earl and Pat Hostetter Martin welcome action and new challenges. In younger years Pat spent a summer working with New York inner-city youth and Earl hitchhiked the country numerous times. Both volunteered for five years of civilian refugee work in Vietnam with Mennonite Central Committee. They met and married there at the peak of the war.

Three children later, they again volunteered to work—this time in the boondock island of Mindanao in the Philippines.

For all their activism, however, Pat and Earl seek always to cultivate the quiet, meditative "inner life." In fact, to find energy for the road, they maintain, one must continually draw from those deep spiritual wells within oneself, and within the lives of people who have known pain and hope. From the very heart of a God who loves the world. Hence, this book.

Currently, Pat and Earl live by the Cocalico Creek near Akron, Pennsylvania, where they share the work of parenting and coordinating the East Asia programs of MCC. They are members of Community Mennonite Church of Lancaster, Pennsylvania.